# LET'S LOOK FOR SHAPES

Bill Gillham *and* Susan Hulme

*Photographs by*
Jan Siegieda

Methuen Children's Books

**round**

Jenny has a round red hoop

**square**

can you see little squares
on the waffles?

**triangle**

Mummy has cut the sandwiches into triangle shapes

**straight**

Daniel and Jenny pull
the rope straight

**zig-zag**

the children's crowns
have zig-zags at the top

**wavy**

the hosepipe makes a wavy line

**oval**

eggs are oval:
this one has a face on it

**diamond**

the trellis makes lots
of diamond shapes

**cross**

a cross is a kiss
when Jenny sends a card

**star**

Baby likes the star
on the Christmas tree

what shapes can *you* see?

LET'S LOOK FOR SHAPES... is one of a series of four books designed to encourage children to *look* for the basic concepts of colour, shape, number and opposites in their everyday world. By talking around the topics illustrated, children will be encouraged to think of other examples and so to develop further their mastery of language and thought, quite apart from the intrinsic pleasure of sharing books with a 'helpful' adult.

Dr Bill Gillham is a well-known educational psychologist and children's author, and senior lecturer in the Department of Psychology at the University of Strathclyde.

Susan Hulme is an experienced infants' teacher, and mother of two young children, with a special interest in pre-school education.

Jan Siegieda is a freelance photographer; these are his first children's books.

*Photograph of rainbow by Walter Leeson.*

*First published in Great Britain 1984*
*by Methuen Children's Books Ltd*
*11 New Fetter Lane, London EC4P 4EE*
*Text copyright © 1984 Bill Gillham and Susan Hulme*
*Photographs copyright © 1984 Bill Gillham and Jan Siegieda*
*Printed in Great Britain by*
*Hazell Watson & Viney Limited,*
*Member of the BPCC Group,*
*Aylesbury, Bucks*

*ISBN 0 416 46190 5*